Faith: No Proof Required
How to Share your Faith with Zero Proof

Faith: No Proof Required
How to Share your Faith with Zero Proof

By Genesis Pilgrim

Genesis Pilgrim
© 2020. All rights reserved.
ISBN: 9781733314558
www.genesispilgrim.com

For the Faithful,

I see it taking form in the clouds, out of reach. Emerging as at the edge of a thread . . . pulling . . . pulsing beams of light:
A distant vision passing from east to west, rising up before the Sun—travelling on its ascension path, leaving plumes in its wake. Like a fell prophet who cuts a cruel channel without concern—intending to desecrate those highest paths established by the Most High.
Its effects dissipate upon us—raining down . . . slow, dry, unnoticed—preceding the groggy awakening of the Earth beneath.

I see clearly: Creation is marred and broken.
I hear it. . . . I feel it. . . .
The Sun and Moon wane behind the restraining veil of the cruel channels. Then they shake themselves free in brilliant splendor—blazing! They wax powerfully, ever faithful, true to the command of the Most High who appointed them on the 4th Day.

My dear friend, what can I say?
How can I comfort you?
I say: Shield your heart from the Tragedy to come. Plant your feet upon rock. Dig deep. Anchor your spirit in that sure foundation. Be refreshed and empowered beneath the brilliance of the firmament. Stand and watch.
See you soon.

Contents

i... **Prelude**

ix... **Introduction**
xi... How to Use this Book
1... Childlike Faith vs. Adult-like Faith
9... Heart Belief vs. Brain Belief
13... Objectivity
17... Truth

19... **Past Generations of Humanity**
21... Claim #1: Human history proves religion is the time-tested means through which societies endure.
25... Claim #2: Ancient humans did not require proof for their beliefs.
29... Claim #3: Ancient humans did not search for religious proof.

33... **Faith in the 21st Century**
35... Claim #4: It is "intellectually dishonest" to claim faith depends on proof.
39... Claim #5: "Proof" is irrelevant to faith.
41... Claim #6: Requirements for "proof" are a result of Western ethnocentrism.

45... **Origins of Faith**
47... Claim #7: Faith rooted in trauma-survival does not require proof.
51... Claim #8: Faith rooted in dreaming does not require proof.

55... Claim #9: Faith rooted in sensory deprivation does not require proof.
59... Claim #10: Requiring "proof" from religion demonstrates ignorance of religion.

63... **The Transcendence of Faith**
65... Claim #11: Faith is designed to be "useful," not "proven."
69... Claim #12: It is unreasonable to require physical proof for spiritual things.
73... Claim #13: The spiritual world is largely unknowable to the physical world, therefore it is unreasonable to demand "proof" for the spiritual.
77... Claim #14: Human perception is limited, so the spiritual world is largely unknowable.
81... Claim #15: Human perception is distracted by biological factors, so the spiritual world is largely unknowable.
85... Claim #16: If an atheist is resolved to live a merely physical life, it makes no sense to ask "proof" for spiritual things.

89... **Faith is Based on One's Desire to Believe—Nothing Further**
91... Claim #17: The undefeatable position: "Faith is believing because I want to believe."
93... Claim #18: Childlike faith gives intellectual freedom to hear others and simply share your faith.
99... Claim #19: The persevering position: Faith is "believing because I want to believe."

101... Claim #20: The unassailable position: Faith is "believing because I want to believe."
105... Claim #21: Childlike faith is the model of Biblical faith (Matt. 18:2-4)

109... **How to Share Your Faith**
111... Example #1: Say this: "I believe in the Bible because I enjoy reading it."
115... Example #2: Say this: "I believe in the Creation story because I like it."
119... Example #3: Say this: "I believe in the Flood because I want to believe in the Flood."
123... Example #4: Say this: "I believe in angels because it helps me when I am scared."
127... Example #5: Say this: "I believe in the spiritual world because it is interesting and helpful."
129... Example #6: Say this: "I believe in the story of Jesus because it is my favorite story."
131... Example #7: Say this: "I believe in the resurrection of Jesus because it is inspiring."
133... Example #8: Say this: "I believe in the afterlife because I am encouraged by its provision of justice."

137... **Conclusions**
139... Claim #22: The best beliefs are time-tested and trustworthy.
143... Faith = No Proof Required

Prelude

The morning air breezed through the lower floor of the house—bringing with it coolness reminiscent of the breaking of Spring. Light blazed through the eastern windows—cascading across the items in the room, as if piercing them with shards of brilliance.

Grandfather often mused to himself on such mornings how the intense sunlight seemed to make the room seem different—as if it causing items to somehow change their form. Mornings were always a time of reflection, where he would pause to revel in the sunrise: perhaps the most basic aspect of existence, yet wondrously profound and awe-inspiring.

On this particular morning, we find Grandfather with his grandson. The young Benjamin squirmed—as children often do, playfully jesting with his grandfather, with limbs tossed about: His mind, advanced as it was, yet nonetheless held captive by his wriggling physical form.

And, rather than chide that simple childish nature, Grandfather accepted the form of Benjamin. So, in their conversations, he was always mindful to allow for Benjamin's inner child to rule his behavior amid their serious discussions.

After all, there was much Grandfather had to teach—to impart to his grandson while he was blessed with the morning sunrises to do so. Although he recoiled at such thoughts, Grandfather held within his mind full self-awareness—realizing after his departure there would be many such sunrises which would cascade upon Benjamin alone.

Thus, Grandfather wielded incredible power within his mind through his sober self-reflection: possessing even the ability to conquer over death itself.

So, why was Benjamin wriggling on this particular morning?

Who knows?

But it might have to do with the thoughts bouncing around in his own mind as he considered the words of Grandfather.

If Benjamin were to speak to you of his grandfather, he would tell you Grandfather often spoke of

Faith: No Proof Required

people long ago. Although his mind was sketchy on the exact details, Benjamin could tell you *much* of humans—especially how they messed up in the past.

And, at this particular moment, Benjamin's mind was wrestling with something Grandfather said about ancient people—called "atheists"—a tribe of which Benjamin was unfamiliar. As Benjamin's limbs jostled about, his mind mingled with the words of Grandfather—somehow still suspended by the beams of light in that room.

In a moment, Benjamin sat up straight—wiggle-free and bright-eyed. The light of the Eastern sky illuminated his face, as if rising only to give occasion for the discussion of this morning.

"Grandpop, why did they do that?"

"Well, you see, those were different times in the ancient world. The laws were different."

"What laws?"

"Well, you know how it is okay for you to think whatever you want in your own mind?"

"Yes. Every person is king over his own mind."

"Exactly, Benjamin. Every person has the right to think whatever he wants. In his own mind, he is the king to decide what he wants to think about." Grandfather was always surprised with the simplicity and ease at which children grasp such concepts.

Grandfather continued, "But in the ancient world, Benjamin, people would try to rule over the minds of other people. They would try to tell other people they *couldn't* think freely in their own minds."

Benjamin was puzzled—and to cope with his inner conflict, he wriggled in his chair. Grandfather was now across the room, reflecting whether or not the discussion was too deep for his young mind. He briefly considered abandoning the conversation, but, when remembering the *Tragedy* which humanity suffered as a result of it, he decided to stay the course. He reasoned he *must* speak to Benjamin about such things. After all, Benjamin's generation might not be fortunate enough to survive if the mistakes of the past are repeated.

Benjamin emerged from his mind and signaled he was ready to continue the conversation.

"So, people would tell other people what they could and couldn't think?"

"Yes, Benjamin."

"Why though? That makes no sense. Why did the ancient people care about what other people were thinking?"

"Well, Ben, for whatever reason, after humans believed in supernatural things for countless generations, some humans—called atheists—thought humans didn't need to believe in supernatural things."

"So, what did they believe in?" Benjamin scoffed. He couldn't imagine people who didn't believe in supernatural things. He thought all humans believed in supernatural things.

"Benjamin, I tell you this because I don't want your generation to make the same mistakes as the ancient people. Somehow the ancient people, around A.D. 2000, began to think of themselves as being only *physical* beings."

Benjamin's head fell forward as he sent a cutting gaze across the room to Grandfather. The threads of sunlight were pushed aside as he replied:

"People who are *just physical*? Like people made of snow or mud?"

"No, Benjamin, real people like us, only they *thought* they were *only physical*." Grandfather paused, considering his words: Just trying to explain the ancients to his grandson made him feel like a madman.

"So, they were people like us, but they *imagined* themselves to be *like* snowmen?"

"Kind of, but instead of snowmen, they imagined themselves to be people without souls or spirits—just people without anything beyond their own bodies."

"Huh!?" Benjamin stood up on the chair, posing like Frankenstein's monster, "Look, Grandfather, I am Arm-and-Leg-Man! All I have is arms and legs. I am like a snowman, but not made of snow. I am just made of arms and legs!"

"Benji, I am being serious though."

Benjamin settled back into his seat.

"The problem wasn't for the atheist people to believe that. People can believe whatever they want."

"Yes, they are kings of their own minds."

"Yes, Ben. The problem happened when the arm-and-leg people convinced many, many people to think *only* about their 'arms and legs.' By doing this, humanity lost its power and when they were tested, they didn't have the ability to survive it."

"It would be boring thinking about myself as just being arms and legs."

"Yes, could you imagine a world, Benjamin, where you are told you can only move things with your hands?"

"No. That's weird," Benjamin looked down at his hands—which looked bizarre now that he thought about it: Thumbs jutted outward, palms up and dangling fingers.

Holding up his hands, Benjamin continued, "Grandpa, I can't imagine what it would be like to think I was *only* this."

"Welcome to the terror which preceded the *Tragedy* in the ancient world, my-son. Humans were persuaded to abandon their own spirits—choosing to see nothing beyond their own physical forms. And, by robbing humanity of its 'spiritual enhancement,' it doomed countless humans when they were tested."

Benjamin nodded.

"Ben, as your generation faces the upcoming *Frontiers*, you must remember *everything* about yourself as a human. Never forsake a part of yourself because that might be the part you need in order to survive."

Introduction

The purpose of this book is to provide a response to 21st Century atheism.

As it is currently, atheism and Christianity are deadlocked in debate—both sides arguing on many different issues. Issues such as "God's existence," "creation," and so on are discussed constantly without agreement.

As I make clear in this book, these debates are the result of misunderstandings concerning the nature of "religion"—as *a system of belief held in the heart of an individual*. And, as I point out, a person's subjective beliefs never need to be "proven" to another. A person is free to hold beliefs within his own mind or heart. He does not need to validate his beliefs to a skeptic.

When understanding this concept—as detailed in the claims of this book—one quickly realizes *all debates* are moot because they begin with a faulty understanding of religion. At its core, religion deals with the *spiritual*—and the spiritual does not bow to the rules of the physical world. Hence, to argue *for* or *against* religion based on "physical things" immediately pulls religion from its actual function.

In other words, when one mingles physical things with belief, then the person is no longer believing *by faith*. The person in this situation then begins believing in merely physical things—"proofs."

So, you must ask yourself, do you believe based on *pure faith*, or do you believe based on *physical things*? As you read further, consider your position carefully. Decide for yourself.

In Christ,

Genesis Pilgrim

How to Use this Book

To lend to its readability, I decided to structure this book based on a series of "claims." Each claim begins with a simple statement—followed by several paragraphs which interact with the claim.

My desire is for believers to use the numbered claims in their discussions with other people—especially those who are curious about Christianity or faith in general. I am convinced you will find these "claims" quite unassailable—which might make them a breath of fresh air when compared to the status quo of *arguments* for and against religion.

My "claims" promote a view of religion which is *purely subjective, personal and heartfelt*. And, when presenting religion in that pure sincerity, you will find it "transcendent"—no longer capable of being debated because religion is beyond all physical things.

So, simply read each "claim." Reflect on what it says. Determine whether you could "poke holes" in the point presented in each claim. If you agree with a claim, maybe you could put a "check" in the margin next to it—signaling to yourself your agreement. Or, jot down the reasons why you disagree. Overall, my goal in writing this book is to assist you in developing your own thoughts.

Later, after you finish this book, if you are able to use my "claims" in your discussions with skeptics, you would find the claims completely change the tone of conversation. Your heartfelt beliefs would no longer be subject to intellectual prodding. Instead, your heartfelt beliefs would be upheld with the dignity they deserve—as a right of your mind to hold precious what it desires.

In this way, my "claims" contribute something most profound to debates: After centuries of debaters trying to force religion to conform to the rules of every physical science, my claims finally permit "religion" to once again become "religion." My claims put religion back atop its rightful pedestal of transcendent reverence.

In generations past, the beliefs of a person were held dearly within their hearts. So, by all means, allow your thoughts of religion to return to that most exalted place within your person. Remove those precious religious thoughts from debate—protecting them from irreverent prodding.

If you desire such heartfelt, sincerely held beliefs, then allow me to renew your mind. I will show you the premiere, foundational form of religion.

I will show you your heart.

Genesis Pilgrim

Faith: No Proof Required

Genesis Pilgrim

Childlike Faith vs. Adult-like Faith

It is clear "adults" have many hang-ups which hinder faith.

So, it is not natural for an adult to "*simply believe.*"

"Adults" are prone to weigh decisions—attempting to position themselves advantageously. Consider how the disciples of Christ argued amongst themselves who was the greatest. Or consider the man whose faith was subdued by his love for money.

However, a child can love without restraint because he is relatively free from such ambitions. Children simply accept and cling to those they love.

Why?

Well, it is ingrained within children to cling to their parents. After all, their survival depends on it. In other words, a child who is more likely to cling closely to his parent, is more likely to be protected and cared for *near* the parent. But a child who does not cling closely to his parent is less likely to benefit from the parent.
Make sense?

Therefore, children are capable of clinging and loving. And this *inclination to cling* enables children to readily walk by faith in God.

Think about it this way . . .

Whereas an adult is inclined to think about the "*whither-to's*" and the "*why-for's*;" a child does not busy himself with such thoughts. A child simply loves his parent—and his parent busies himself with the task of making food and providing for the child.

So, how does God want us to relate to Him?

As our Father.

The Lord Jesus invited the little children to be brought to Him (Matt. 19:13-15). While adults near Christ strained at thoughts of their own greatness and how to "earn" God's blessing, the Lord Jesus upheld *childlike faith as ideal* (Matt. 18:1-5).

Therefore, God desires us to simply cling to Him. We are called to have simple faith—leaving to God the "*whither-to's*" and the "*why-for's*."

So, why does this matter?

Well, consider how "faith" is regarded in the 21st Century. Ask yourself if faith is discussed in this way . . .

Is "childlike faith" upheld as the ideal? Or do we promote thoughts of adult-like intellectualism?

Quite sadly it is the latter.

Truly, in the 21st Century, faith is often mingled with intellectual thoughts—so grievously as if to convince us, quite contrary to the teachings of Jesus, that we must have "reasons" to believe what we do.

In fact, there are many apologetic ministries which are built upon intellectualism—promoting the thought that we must reason with our faith. And, as they suppose, if we cannot "prove" our faith then we cannot have faith.

For example, consider the creation story in the Bible. . . .

Now, a child who believes in the Genesis creation story, *simply believes*. No extra "proof" is required.

But an adult who believes in the Genesis creation story is told he should be capable of stating "proofs" for his belief. And, it is implied if he cannot state enough convincing "proofs," then he should abandon his belief in the Genesis creation story. Sadly, many who follow this model of proof-based beliefs have chosen to forsake the churches in which they were raised.

Why?

Well, when children are raised in a spiritual environment that promotes reliance on "proofs," then when they fail to accept "proofs" for themselves, they abandon Christian faith. Therefore, "proof-based" Christian organizations might be doing more harm than good by promoting the idea that young people must have physical proofs for what they maintain in their hearts.

Consider this carefully.

And, as my book will point out below, having adult-like faith leads to many problems—ultimately making the adult hold positions which are intellectually dishonest—if indeed he chooses to maintain his beliefs despite contrary "proofs" (see page 35).

Consider this carefully as well. Then you will clearly understand why many young people turn away from the churches in which they were raised.

So, what is the best way—the simple faith of the *child* or the intellectual, proof-driven faith of the *adult*?

Clearly, according to the Lord Jesus, the faith of the child is better (Matt. 18:1-5)! After all, a child's faith is unshakable. They simply cling and love—with no need for reason. The love of the child is purely subjective and heartfelt. It requires no reason. Love is simply there and maintained by the child's desire to hold it.

However, the adult's faith is wavering—as he is ever tossed about by his intellect (Matt. 11:25). It is no wonder when young adults are told their religious beliefs rely on physical proofs that they forsake their religion when they stop accepting those physical "proofs."

Therefore, in practice, we discover the truth in Jesus' teaching. In fact, childlike faith is much more enduring than adult-like faith. And in this way, childlike faith is preferred—as it gives an individual the highest chances of perseverance under *all* circumstances.

After all, if one's religion is purely subjective, based only on his own desire to believe, then nothing outside his mind can persuade him to depart from his belief. In other words, the more subjective and childlike your faith, the more powerful it becomes!

Whereas a child is "free" to love and cling without regard for reason; an adult is held captive by his reason—thinking he must "prove" a thing before he upholds it in his heart. A child believes *subjectively*; an adult thinks *objectively*.

As my book points out, childlike faith has *always* been the proper model of Bible faith. Always.

Indeed, it is most foreign to mingle intellectualism with faith.

After the Lord Jesus rose from the dead, Thomas doubted—saying he would not believe unless he felt for himself the nail marks. Later the Lord Jesus appeared to Thomas and he believed.
So, what was the conclusion?
Were readers encouraged to adopt the attitude of Thomas—refusing to believe unless receiving *physical proof*?
Absolutely not.
Although Thomas needed physical proof, John encourages us to "believe" *without physical proof* (John 20:24-31). And, by doing so—simply believing in what is written—we can have eternal life in Jesus' Name.

Sadly, however, Christian apologetics have adopted wholesale the *adult-like* method of Thomas, rather than the *childlike* belief of John. In the 21st Century you are told you must have "physical proof" for what you believe. And in this way, 21st Century Christian apologetics is guilty of error—leading many down an objective path where they dissuade themselves from spiritual volition.

    In conclusion: The church must simply *believe*—with childlike faith. At your core, your belief must be child-like and purely subjective. You must understand what that means.
    Of course, we look forward to Heaven—when we see Christ face to face and feel the nail marks for ourselves. But as it is now—in your Earthly walk—your faith requires *absolutely nothing* physical.

    No proof is required for heartfelt, childlike faith.

Heart Belief vs. Brain Belief

Quite interestingly, when one cites the "heart" as the place of religious belief, they are in effect promoting childlike faith over adult-like faith.

What do I mean?

Well, where does *natural thinking* take place?

The brain.

In other words, to say a person "thinks with his heart," would be *naturally* incorrect. That is, a person thinks only with his brain.

So, why does religion often emphasize the importance of the heart? After all, *natural thinking* does not occur within the heart.

The answer: Belief by definition is *beyond the natural*.

Belief is *supernatural*—which means it transcends, or is beyond, all things which are natural. Belief is not based on natural or physical things.
Therefore, the mechanism of *supernatural belief* is a *supernatural means*. This is why beliefs are said to be "in the heart"—a supernatural location symbolized by the core of our person.

Cool, huh?

So, to say one believes something "in his heart" is to imply the *transcendence* of religion.

If beliefs were based on merely physical proofs, there would be no reason for us to hold beliefs in a location other than our physical *brains*.
But since beliefs are not dependent on anything physical, they are rooted in something which is beyond all physical things. This is why we say beliefs are stored in the spiritual *heart* of a person—a location completely beyond the reach of all physical things. The physical world may crumble around us, but our *heartfelt beliefs*

would endure all things—being unshaken by any physical trial or hardship, or even physical death.

Get it?

Thus, we see the common reference to the "heart" as the seat of belief as a sharp rebuke to the 21st Century mingling of "proofs" and religion. True religion is stored in the transcendent heart or "mind"—which is different than the physical brain. And, from that location in the spiritual heart, the religion of a person does not bow to anything in the physical world—including demands for "proof."

So, I invite you most *heartily* (pun intended!) to "believe with your heart," rather than your physical brain. By doing so you will anchor yourself beyond the physical veil of our world.

Don't push and cram the *supernatural* within the bounds of the *natural*. Don't force your beliefs to fit in your *brain* by memorizing lists of physical "proofs."

Instead, follow the counsel of the Lord Jesus and adopt *childlike faith*. Put faith *within your heart*—far beyond the reach of anything physical. This is how you will gain the ability to persevere all things.

Objectivity

To say something is "objective" means it can be validated to be true—at least within its own system.

For example, although one might not believe in the Bible, the truths contained within that book hold objectivity. In other words, one can say things which are *objectively true* in the Bible—such as "*God created the Earth,*" "*Christ died and rose from the grave,*" "*Moses performed miracles,*" and so on.

Therefore, the Bible contains objective truth within itself—because the events described therein are true within it.

However, when one chooses to believe in the Bible, they should do so *subjectively*—meaning they should stand upon their own desire to believe.

To say a belief is "subjective," means it is personal and needs no validation beyond the individual who holds it.

Thus, by taking a purely subjective, childlike position of faith, the Bible-believer removes all requirements for objectivity.

In other words, the reason why Christian apologists have debates with atheists is because they both wrest their opponents to gain control of *objectivity*—the right to say something is "true" in the wide assessment of the entire world. An example of this includes Christian apologists arguing to *objectively* prove the Flood with geology.

My position, however, is that outward objectivity <u>does not matter to your faith</u>.

Why in the world should you care if the world accepts what you believe?

The "world" is the "world" because it chooses to remain in unbelief. Therefore, you should not seek the world's approval.

Your faith should be wholly subjective—trusting in the Bible with childlike faith. Within the Bible itself, its teachings are objectively true, but you do not need to pummel the world with debate arguments. Simply declare your heartfelt genuine beliefs—telling others how Christ has blessed your own heart and life. By doing so, you will put yourself beyond all arguments and debates.

    You have a right to believe.

    Your mind is free.

    Your heart is your own.

    Do not let anyone convince you otherwise.

Truth

My position is that heartfelt, childlike faith does not require proof. A person simply believes in Jesus because he wants to believe in Jesus.

So, I have heard it said, *"Aren't you concerned with knowing what is true?"*

Of course, I am concerned with knowing what is true!

But my heart is not governed by what society determines to be "true." Rather, I believe in Jesus because I want to believe in Jesus—with the faith of a child.

I am free to investigate historical claims and archaeological data, but I do so with the realization that my faith ultimately does not depend on those things. My faith is based on my heartfelt desire to trust Jesus. And, for that, no proof is required.

Past Generations of Humanity

Claims #1-3 below interact with how religion (in general) served a vital role in *ancient humanity*. Additionally, these claims put forth the fact that the religions of the ancients were not based on "proofs." Rather religion was based on their own *subjective* minds.

In other words, religious ancients did not base their beliefs on archeological "proofs." They did not need to undergo expeditions to unearth things to "prove" what they believed. Instead, *they simply believed*.

In our ancient past, religious humans were never inclined to state long lists of "proofs" for what they believed.

They *simply believed what they believed*.
No strings attached.

Genesis Pilgrim

Claim #1
Human history proves religion is the time-tested means through which societies endure.

Discussion

To properly understand religion (in general), we must return to the foundation of humanity.

In the 21st Century, humans are prone to be ethnocentric and provincial—imagining themselves the supreme form of humanity, the pinnacle of human history.

Yet, in our analysis of the many millennia of humanity, we find religion ubiquitously intertwined with *all* enduring human societies. Therefore, atheism is not the enduring form of mankind. Rather, the religious man is the truest form—thoroughly attested by all historical records.

Yes, ancient people believed *different* things—but they all believed in something nonetheless. Therefore, it is more natural to our human form to believe in *something* rather than *nothing*.

The form of religion I describe—the one where a person subjectively believes—is the foundational form of religion.

All ancient human societies—at least the ones that survived long enough to make records—were *all* religious. Sure, there were probably *some* atheist people sprinkled in there. But atheist people have never built enduring, successful human societies. Never. And, it remains to be seen what atheism will do to harm our current societies.

This is why I recoil whenever I hear 21st Century atheists deride tribes of the Ancient Near East as "ignorant goat-herders." Indeed, throughout the parade of generations upon the Earth, irony offers a reversal: Whereas the people of the Ancient Near East produced successful civilizations, which competed well and maintained their existence; atheism is a system which has never produced an enduring society.

Never.

Therefore, although we might disagree with our ancient ancestors on many points, we should avoid deriding them. After all, those ancient religious people survived while many others did not. So, we certainly cannot label ancient survivors as "ignorant." Clearly, they were the most adept and fit in their generations—demonstrating the unique contributions of religion (in general) to the advancement of human societies.

Since we have no record of enduring ancient atheist societies, this means religion was a necessary component for survival. *Religion has ever been the egg in the brownie mix—helping everything stick together.*

Thus, irony it seems, keeps *selecting* atheism for decline; whereas religious humans are *selected* for survival.

In my book, Survival of the Superstitious: How Religion Helped Ancient Humans Survive, I discuss this in detail. History shows us quite clearly that religion was the most beneficial enhancement of humans—enabling them to survive the otherwise un-survivable. Birds have wings; cats have claws; but humans have religion—which accelerates our ability to think in abstract terms, thereby serving as a catalyst for *all* intelligent thinking and creativity.

Human history demonstrates the "fittest" version of humanity is the "religious human." Because, no matter where we look in human history, "religious societies" were the ones which endured long-term.

Therefore, by deriding the *religious ancients*, a person merely demonstrates his ethnocentric, provincial ignorance of human history. Indeed, in the ancient world our best hope of survival would be to find ourselves in a society governed by religious humans.

Religious societies survived.

Atheist societies didn't make it.

Therefore, human history demonstrates religion is the time-tested means through which societies endure.

Let me leave you with this thought . . .

In all human history, atheism never created enduring societies. So, what do you think will happen to *your society* as it is increasingly brought under the control of atheism?

The endurance of societies depends on the spirituality of its citizens. History demonstrates this.

Claim #2
Ancient humans did not require proof for their beliefs.

Discussion

The recent trend among 21st Century humans is to require "proof" for religious beliefs. In other words, when a person says they believe something, a skeptic often asks them to "prove" his belief is "true." Then, when the person cannot offer "acceptable" physical proof, the two argue with one another.

Sound familiar?

However, for all of human history, there was never such a requirement for "proof." Indeed, the requirement to "prove" faith is a recent addition amid the insanity of the decades leading up to the 21st Century.

For example, could you imagine approaching an ancient Norse warrior and asking him to "prove" the existence of his "god?" It makes no sense to consider such things.

Why would an ancient person care about "proving" his faith to someone who doesn't want to believe in it?

If a skeptic has no desire to believe, then what's the point asking for explanations?

In this way we sense the complete futility in such conversations. People should be left as the ancients—to either choose to believe or refrain. But demanding proof for the beliefs of another person merely serves as a catalyst for pointless arguments.

In some cases in the ancient world, validation might have been required of a person making extraordinary claims. An example would be the expectation for religious leaders—like Moses and the Lord Jesus—to perform miracles.

But a miracle itself does not serve as "proof" for a *whole* religion. A miracle only serves to offer slight validation to the individual. After all, a miracle cannot show you the events of Creation itself—how God created the Earth, events of the Afterlife and so on. So, even miracles were not intended to "prove" the *entire* religion of the miracle-worker.

Therefore, the idea that religious people must "prove" their beliefs to be "true" is nonsense. There is no precedent for this in human history.

So, why—after countless generations of human have existed—does atheism think it makes sense to require "proof" for religion?

Ancient humans were not required to state "proofs" for their beliefs. Nor should religious humans in the 21st Century be placed under such a burden.

People are *free* to believe what they desire. They do not need to justify their beliefs to others.

Faith = No proof required.

Claim #3
Ancient humans did not search for religious proof.

Discussion

For human history immemorial—extending countless generations—religion has existed without the requirement for proof. People simply believed what they wanted to—whether for personal reasons or as a part of their affinity for their social clan.

The ability to investigate is a very recent addition to humanity.

Mind you, *literacy itself* is a very recent addition to humanity. Myriads of humans have lived and died without the ability to interact with anything beyond their immediate surroundings.

Yet, *now* humans are being told they need "proof" for everything? Humans have never lived to such an absolute standard!

People have always been *free to believe* in what helps them *survive each day*. People "believed" what they desired to believe (individually, socially or whatever).

People in the ancient world didn't search for rocks and icons to "prove" stuff. They simply believed or they didn't.

Don't think about "religion" in terms of a televangelist who is peddling his nonsense. Think about religion (in general)—which has helped humans survive for millennia. The form of religion I describe is the one which humans have held for time immemorial: *Faith which is unashamedly subjective and personal.*

Unlike the expectations atheism heaps on the religious in its demands for proof, people never attached the need for "proof" to support their religious beliefs. People who were barely "scraping by" and struggling to subsist off their lands didn't set out to "prove" their religion by archaeology and travelling to far off places. "Proving" their religion was not a thing they did.

Likewise, it lacks precedent with *all human history* for atheism to demand proof for modern religion when ancient believers were never held to this standard.

Therefore, it would be most prudent to return to the foundation of religion. Religion is a means of survival—whereby an individual gains the ability to conceptualize his worldview in a way which is inspiring. Thus, religion is purely subjective and personal—being held with childlike faith in the heart of an individual.

Why in the world would such a precious thing need to be "proven" to a skeptic? Ancient humans never opened their precious beliefs to such brutal scrutiny. Neither should we.

Ancient humans did not need to "search for proof" for their beliefs.
Neither do we.

Faith in the 21st Century

Claims #4-6 interact with how faith is regarded in the 21st Century. These claims are *food-for-thought*—helping the reader to challenge common teachings about religious faith.

I hope you enjoy them! . . .

Genesis Pilgrim

Claim #4
It is "intellectually dishonest" to claim faith depends on proof.

Discussion

Consider this statement . . .

"I believe (x) because of (y)."

If I take this position, I am telling you that my belief system (x), depends on the "proof" of (y).

Get it?

But by me making such a statement, I am directly implying that if you, as a skeptic, are capable of "disproving" (y), then I will concede—or give up—my belief in (x).

(Make sure you understand this because if you are a Christian this is a major source of the disconnect you have with atheists.)

The fact, however, is that your faith (x) does not depend on (y).

How do I know this?

Because, even if we got rid of (y), *you would still believe* what you desire to believe.

For example, let's say I were to tell you this . . .

"I believe in the (resurrection) because of the (empty tomb)."

This statement would tell you my faith in the resurrection of Jesus *depends* on the "proof" of the empty tomb. But by declaring the "empty tomb" to be "proof" for my belief, I am logically conceding that if you somehow disprove the "empty tomb," I will completely abandon my belief in the resurrection.

Now, Christian, by declaring your faith rests on certain "proofs" you are dishonestly telling the world you would abandon your *entire faith* if those proofs could be disproven.

And, we know this is not the case.

Surely, your *entire faith* does not rely on a couple "proofs"—does it? Rather your faith is rooted in *your own desire to hold belief within your heart*. As long as you desire to hold your faith, you do so—by the power of God. Therefore, your own faith is not based on "proofs" *whatsoever*.

But if your faith truly depends on "proofs," I pity you. Because this is *adult-like faith*—and this leads to all types of wavering as a person is tossed about by intellectual arguments and debates.

And, more disastrously, if your faith depends on "proofs," you make yourself vulnerable to shipwreck. After all, whenever you are convinced to abandon *any* of your proofs, your faith becomes increasingly more endangered—ever closer to being abandoned altogether.

So, what is the solution?

The solution is to adopt *childlike faith*—which will ensure your beliefs will *persevere all things*.

According to the teachings of the Bible, the followers of Christ persevere all things. The faithful remain true to Christ no matter what the world throws at them. Therefore, your faith should not depend on "proof."

Rather, your faith should depend only on your personal desire to maintain that belief. This is how "beliefs" work—and have always worked.

For example, if you believe in the resurrection, the only reason why you should believe in the resurrection is because you *desire* to believe in the resurrection!

Leave aside all lists of "proof" and simply believe in the resurrection with child-like faith: *Believe in the resurrection because <u>you want to believe</u> in the resurrection.*

Does this sound too simple?

Perhaps . . . but it is true.

Therefore, we see *adult-like faith* is intellectually dishonest and endangers the faith of those who depend on proofs. Whereas, *childlike faith* is heartfelt, personal and persevering.

In other words, a person with *adult-like faith* can be dissuaded from their beliefs—quite easily at times.

But a person with *childlike faith* can never be dissuaded from <u>his own heart</u>. Thus, childlike faith is superior to adult-like faith (Matt. 18:1-5).

Claim #5
"Proof" is irrelevant to faith.

Discussion

To the person who recognizes the foundational-level understanding of religious belief, "proof" does not matter. To the man who bases his life on sincere belief in his heart, he does not need to depend on "proofs" for things like the resurrection, the life of Jesus, authorship of the Bible, etc. He simply has faith—upholding in his heart his own personal beliefs.

Humans are creatures who *decide for themselves* what they believe. They choose to follow those things which inspire them. This is the true form of religion held by humans throughout all history.

Adding the requirement for "proofs" is foreign to this foundational form of faith.

Think about it: Faith does not depend on "proof."

Claim #6
Requirements for "proof" are a result of Western ethnocentrism.

Discussion
European and American societies are centered upon democratic principles: We vote; we have jury trials.

As a result, people in the West are inclined to also view religious issues *democratically*—supposing that society itself, or a large group of people, has the ability to determine by "vote" what is true and what is false.

Therefore, we see clearly the over-emphasis on "proof" is a result of our Western culture. In other words, Western societies tend to treat everything as a "vote."

But when looking at all of human history, we see people "believed" what they needed to in order to survive. So, religious belief is foundationally based on survival and what one "wants to/has to" believe to survive.

Survival is not guaranteed. Religious beliefs granted ancient people who were otherwise hopeless, hope.

Once a person realizes this, all the "debates" go away.
Contrary to our Western presuppositions, religion is not a thing voted upon. Nor is it something competed against.

Instead, people *believe to survive*. They believe what they need to/want to in order to survive.

Thus, when we realize our Western presupposition, it makes little sense to banter about religion on debate stages—as if popular opinion has any bearing on issues of the heart.
People are free to believe what they desire to believe. It has always been this way, and it always will be. Heartfelt religious beliefs need no validation. Nor do they need to be defended in debate.

Faith: No Proof Required

Origins of Faith

In Claims #7-10 below, I present the ancient foundations of religion (in general). As I explain, when we recognize the importance of dreams, trauma and other similar occurrences in religions, it negates requirements for physical "proof." Religion is spiritual; not physical.

So, as you will see, the very formation of religious thinking precludes "proof."

Enjoy! . . .

Claim #7
Faith rooted in trauma-survival does not require proof.

Discussion

People go through horrific things—wars, violence, starvation and so on.

In its root form, the purpose of religion is that it allows the individual to survive tragedy.

Think of a person who is imprisoned in a pit. He is surrounded by physical horror and there is nothing *physical* in which he can rightly place his hope.

In order to survive, this person must develop the ability to "see" outside the pit. He must find a way to have *hope*—fixing his mind on good things ahead.

This is the foundational root of religion. When people go through horrific things, religion has always been used to help people muster the ability to somehow survive.

Get it?

So, when thinking about religion, approach it from this perspective. In its root form, religion is most helpful because it grants people the hope they need to survive.

Now here is the insanity of atheism's criticism of religion . . .

In the 21st Century, atheism tells Christians they must "prove" what they believe to be "true."

This is nonsense. And there is no precedent for it in the ancient world.

Imagine the insanity of this similar scenario . . .

Think again of our man who is imprisoned in the pit. Now, in the midst of his suffering, the man recently developed the habit of singing hymns—using religion to transport his mind to visions of Heaven and hope.

Now, could you imagine what would happen if an atheist approached that man, asking him to "prove" if his songs were "true."

It doesn't make any sense to imagine such things. The man in the pit is not concerned with the opinions of a comfortable person who criticizes his religion. To the man in the pit, his mind is fixed on surviving each moment. And, in that way, his religion is quite truly his only *hope* of survival.

Therefore, faith rooted in trauma-survival does not require proof. Its purpose is survival, not skeptical debate.

Claim #8
Faith rooted in dreaming does not require proof.

Discussion

Humans dream—vividly. And, even when we awaken, we *remember* dreams.

Heck, even when we are fully awake, we *day-dream* all the time—constantly fixing our minds on non-present things and ideas.

In fact, one could say humans live more *within our minds* than we do in the physical world. We are constantly thinking about things beyond our surroundings. And we are constantly engaged in self-talk within our own minds.

So, it makes sense to see spiritual beliefs as an extension of this propensity for dreaming. And, when we consider that *all* ancient human societies were religious, it is likely religion was a catalyst for the development of all abstract thinking, imagination, creativity and logic—because to participate in any of those things involves humans thinking of *non-present* things.

So, what's my point?

Imagine the insanity of the following scenario . . .

When a man awakens from a dream, he recounts the vivid details of his dream to another person.

Now, here's the question . . .

Do you think it would make sense for the listener to demand "proof" from the dreamer?

(This is too ridiculous to consider.) But imagine the listener starts prodding the dream-teller . . .

"Your dream isn't real!"

"You can't prove that really happened!"

"I don't believe you dreamed that!"

Yet, this is exactly what 21st Century atheism does with religious people. And it is equally insane. Within the mind of the religious person, his beliefs exist as *dreams and visions*—for which no justification or proof is required.

Therefore, faith is like a precious childlike dream held within the heart of a person. Indeed, the Bible makes many references to religious dreams—thoroughly recognizing it as a means through which God communicates with people.

It makes no sense to tear apart a person for what they dream in the visions of the night or throughout the day. So, why in the world would someone ever dare challenge the religious thoughts of another?

A person is just as *free to believe* as they are *free to dream*. Thus, faith does not require proof.

Claim #9
Faith rooted in sensory deprivation does not require proof.

Discussion

Some religious beliefs may be rooted in sensory deprivation.

In other words, when people would pray in secluded locations, darkness and other factors could have heightened their perceptions in other ways. Therefore, in many religions, certain *locations* are held as sacred—likely due to the changes in perception people may have experienced in such locations.

An example of this would be the use of caves for some religious events. Or the idea of withdrawing into the wilderness or atop a mountain to commune with God.

To avoid discussing this aspect of sensory deprivation too much, suffice it to say that just as it would be silly to ask a person to "prove" a religious dream, so it would be silly to ask a person to "prove" a *certain experience.*

What does it matter anyway?

If a person wants to believe something and uphold a particular experience as special in his own heart, who are you tell him he's *wrong*?

Yet, atheism does this with the resurrection appearances of the Lord Jesus—demanding "proof" from believers who hold these stories precious.

Could you imagine the insanity of going to a funeral—just to tell mourners "they have no proof" for thinking their "loved one" lives on?

It would be an absurd cruelty. But in its brutal treatment of ancient people, atheism tramples upon the grief of the mourning disciples in its demand for "proof."

So, if a person prays and God helps him in his prayers, who is anyone to tear down those dearly held beliefs?

People are free to withdraw—imploring God to speak to them in their time of seclusion. And, to the person who is inspired in the wilderness of grief or self-searching, it makes no sense to besiege him with skepticism upon his return.

People are free to believe what they desire within their hearts. The objections of others are irrelevant.

Therefore, faith rooted in sensory deprivation does not require proof.

Claim #10
Requiring "proof" from religion demonstrates ignorance of religion.

Discussion
By the atheist requiring "proof" from the suffering religious person, the atheist demonstrates he does not understand the root form of religion.

Since religion is based on trauma-survival, dreams and sensory deprivation, it makes no sense to force it into something it was never intended to be.

The root form of religion, as I point out, is not based on "proof." Rather, religion (in general) is a tool used by individuals and societies to help them survive hardship.

Therefore, those who are inclined to treat religion as a thing to be physically-attested demonstrate they lack understanding of "religion." Religion is a purely subjective, spiritual venture which takes place in the heart of an individual. As such, physical demonstrations should not be required.

A person is free to hold his own beliefs within his heart.

Faith: No Proof Required

Genesis Pilgrim

The Transcendence of Faith

The physical world and the spiritual world are like apples and oranges. They are different.

Thus, is it reasonable to suppose spiritual things can be perceived by the physical world?

No.

Indeed, it is unreasonable for atheism to demand physical proof for things which are transcendent to the physical world.

In Claims #11-16 below I explain how faith is elusive to those without faith—simply because faith speaks about a world *beyond* physical perception.

I hope you enjoy! . . .

Claim #11
Faith is designed to be "useful," not "proven."

Discussion

Everything has a purpose. Demanding something beyond a thing's purpose is ridiculous.

For example, I don't use my laptop computer to wash my dishes.
And, I don't use my car to bake brownies.

Reflect on what I am saying.

Yet, despite the intended purpose of religion, atheism demands something from "religion" for which it was never designed.

The atheist is the person who throws a laptop into a sink of dishes, then complains the computer isn't smart enough to figure it out.

Think about it . . .

Religion (in general) is designed to help people survive.

In some cases, we can picture tribal leaders in the ancient world developing beliefs to protect their people. By telling them about ghosts in the nighttime forest, they protected their believing citizens from all potential risks encountered in the nighttime forest—like hypothermia, getting lost, bandits, etc. Therefore, the original purpose of religious stories was linked to community survival.

So, when religious stories are designed for the purpose of inspiring, protecting and unifying people, how much sense does it make to demand from religion something which is beyond its design?

Just like the laptop—which wasn't made to wash dishes, so also religious stories were not made to be technical textbooks containing time-stamped video evidence that interacts through the filtered mind of the skeptic.

Religion was designed to help people survive; Religion was not designed to conform to the expectations of 21st Century atheism.

Like the laptop computer, religion must be understood based on its design. Therefore, since religion was designed to be practical to individuals, it does not need to be proven.

In Western culture, people are raised with the false perception as if everything must be "voted" upon—and somehow mass consensus equals "truth." But religion does not bow to such Western presupposition.

Faith is subjective and personal. And, as such, heartfelt, personal faith is immune to scrutiny. A person believes as *he desires to believe*. He requires no stamp of approval or validation to maintain the beliefs of his heart.

Thus, religion is designed to be useful to the individual, not proven.

Claim #12
It is unreasonable to require *physical* proof for *spiritual* things.

Discussion
By definition, *spiritual things* are *spiritual*.

I know this is basic stuff, but it needs to be explained.

Think about it this way . . .

If a *spiritual* being (like an angel) exists, then his primary existence is in a plane of existence outside of the *physical* plane. The angel might *briefly* touch into our physical plane of existence—but his spiritual essence is something *beyond* it.

Get it?

If you don't understand, consider the concept of the "**tesseract**" in physics. Even from a physical perspective, an item which holds extra dimensions "beyond" the physical plane, cannot wholly exist in the physical plane. This means this concept is fully acknowledged by physics.

So, bear with me for a moment . . .

If there are spiritual beings, their forms are expressed through different dimensions. For this reason, they do not primarily exist on the physical plane.

So, how does it make sense to require "physical proof" for a spiritual thing that just barely intersects our physical world?

It doesn't make sense.

Therefore, a person is either left with the decision to believe in supernatural things or not. No proof is required, nor does it make sense to ask for proof. Either choose to believe in things *beyond* the physical plane or don't.

In other words, since spiritual things would exist beyond our physical ability to perceive them, it is irrational to require physical proof for them.

If a person believes in a spiritual thing, it is most likely impossible for him to show you that spiritual thing on our physical plane of existence—simply due to physics.

Therefore, it is unreasonable to expect *physical* proof for *non-physical, spiritual* things.

Claim #13
The spiritual world is largely unknowable to the physical world, therefore it is unreasonable to demand "proof" for the spiritual.

Discussion

Remember our discussion of the tesseract on page 70. In physics it is acknowledged that if a physical construct (like a tesseract) has dimensions beyond our limitations of perception, we will not be able to see it fully.

Borrowing from this physics concept, we can be certain that spiritual things—if presumed to exist—are largely unknowable in the physical plane.

What is the implication?

Think about the concept of the Afterlife . . .

Although we are free to "believe what we desire" during our physical lives, if our existence somehow continues beyond the physical, it is obvious our perceptions will likewise change. And, with a change in form—from physical to non-physical—there will be things which will be surprises.

Why do I say this?

Because, it is impossible to know *everything* about what is beyond the physical veil. Just as one could not fully perceive tesseract items, one would not be able to fully perceive *spiritual* things.

Clearly humans cannot fully see what is beyond their own limitations of perception—so it is unreasonable to demand a Christian to "prove" his beliefs in spiritual things.

Will we be surprised by the Afterlife in the spiritual world?

Absolutely—of course there would be differences and experiences beyond our present ability to perceive.

Certainly, a transition from physical form to spiritual form would necessitate a change in our ability to perceive. This being the case, frankly, we cannot know *everything* about what exists beyond our current physical plane.

Therefore, it is quite unreasonable to ask for *physical* proofs for *non-physical* things. Thus, no proof is required for faith.

Claim #14
Human perception is limited, so the spiritual world is largely unknowable.

Discussion
Human perception exists in a very narrow range.

For example, when considering our sense of hearing, a human possesses only a fraction of the hearing ability possessed by cats.

When considering our perception of smell, humans possess only a fraction of the smell ability of dogs.

And, when considering the vision perception of humans, we possess only a very limited ability. If you are unsure about this, use a pair of military-grade infrared night-vision goggles.

So, do you still trust your senses?

Even if one could prove spiritual things using physical proofs, are your senses reliable enough for you to accept what they tell you?

In other words, even if you were to "see" an angel, would you trust your eyes? Or would you dismiss what you saw as imagination?

Thus, knowing your incredible sense limitations, does it make sense to deny spiritual things?

For example, even if an angel were to appear physically, we could only "see" him if he was in the *light range* perceived by our eyes. And, even if an angel were to speak to us, we could only "hear" him if he spoke in a perceivable *decibel range*.

Humans cannot fully perceive *physical* things. So, how is it reasonable for such sense-blind humans to boldly deride what might exist *beyond* the physical plane of our existence? We cannot fully perceive the *physical* things around us, yet people are so bold to ask for proof of *spiritual* things.

In fact, physical human perception is so dull, you could have many things occurring on the physical plane mere feet away from you. Yet, you might not perceive events because of your limitations: An angel could bump into you, tap you on the shoulder and whisper in your ear . . . and you *perceive* nothing.

Therefore, humans would be most wise to avoid deriding spiritual things—which exist beyond our physical plane. Even if a spiritual thing could be shown us, it is most likely our senses would preclude perception.

Therefore, human perception limitations demonstrate it is unreasonable to demand "proof" for spiritual things.

Claim #15
Human perception is distracted by biological factors, so the spiritual world is largely unknowable.

Discussion
Earlier on page 73, we discussed the physics concept of the tesseract—demonstrating how spiritual things would be largely *unknowable*.

So, extending this concept further, consider this statement: Humans cannot trust their perceptions to fully discern truth.

Why?

Well, your ability to perceive is constantly clouded by your biology.

For example, if a person is exhausted or tired, his perception will vary from a person who is well-rested. Or if a person is hungry, his perception will vary from a person who is not.

But this gets very complicated—to the point that *human perceptions as a whole are completely out of control* and we don't know it.

For example, consider the constant yo-yo experienced in insulin as a result of the diet of a person. Or consider sex drive. Or consider the fact that people routinely flood their dopamine reward system through social media and other electronic means—giving themselves a constant stream of feelings inconsistent with their actual physical surroundings.

What's my point?

My point is that humans are rarely *level-headed*. Instead, the consciousness of the average 21st Century human rides within a rocketing rollercoaster—constantly tossed about by biological function. The 21st Century human is indeed so captured by these intense biological functions, one could argue—quite accurately—that even if he were to witness a partial appearance of a tesseract-like object, he might not even possess the level-headed perception required to *sense* it.

In other words, even if an angel were to tap you on your shoulder and speak to you, it is likely your many other biological functions would preclude your perception.

Get it?

Have you ever wondered why religions often emphasize *self-denial*—through prayer, fasting and meditation?

Think of a computer. Imagine opening up 100 different programs and windows on your computer, then complaining because your computer is "slow."

This stuff is common sense: While a person is riding on a dopamine-driven, insulin-fueled roller coaster, it is doubtful he would ever have the level perspective to perceive a "tesseract" item. Therefore, if a person wants to glimpse "tesseracts," or spiritual things, the first step would require the person to slow all his biological "programs" to a minimum to allow his senses to sharpen.

Make sense?

So, if you want to have a chance at perceiving something beyond your mere physical circumstances, start by "closing" as many "programs" as possible on your biological "computer." Get yourself *level* on this physical plane. Then you might have a change to sense the gentle fluttering of tesseracts which exist *beyond* it.

Thus, in this discussion, we see human perception is limited by biological factors. As long as a human lacks the discipline to control his own physical body, it makes no sense to banter about what exists beyond.

For example, if a person has lived his entire life subsisting on sugar, he has no idea what it "feels" like to live without sugar. Thus, *everything he has ever experienced* has been perceived through the filter of the effects of sugar.

Of course, this is only one example. But we know for certain that biological factors can cause changes in perception. Therefore, in the quest to determine objective truth, one would be wise to take into account biological factors. It might be that spiritual disciplines—such as self-denial, fasting, prayer and meditation—serve as requisite means through which someone experiences "spiritual" things beyond our physical plane.

Claim #16
If an atheist is resolved to live a merely physical life, it makes no sense to ask "proof" for spiritual things.

Discussion

Keeping in mind the physics concept of the tesseract, it is acknowledged that humans would only see a small "part" of any such item which briefly intersects our physical plane of existence.

Therefore, we accept it is impossible for us to know *everything* about planes of existence beyond our own. At best, we could receive brief glimpses of tesseract items—but by definition we could not see the entire item *all at once* on our physical plane.

It is impossible for humans to fully know everything about what exists beyond our physical plane of existence.

And, even if a human "fully knew" everything of the tesseract planes of existence beyond our physical plane, it is likely there would be no means to accurately describe such things to humans whose minds are held captive by the physical plane.

Get it?

Please make sure you understand.

Therefore, if a physical-plane human, like an atheist, is content to live as a *merely physical being*—thinking only of physical things—then he should abandon pursuing knowledge of tesseract-things. They are unknowable anyway.

So, what's the point of atheism demanding "proof" from a Christian?

There is no point.

The tesseract planes of existence are by definition *largely unknowable* and *most likely indescribable*. Thus, it is unreasonable for an atheist to demand answers for the unknowable and indescribable.

Moreover, it is unreasonable for an atheist to be content living as a merely physical being, yet prodding questions about unknowable tesseract dimensions. What is the purpose? After all, the atheist has already committed to a purely physical-existence.

Is such an atheist driven to ask questions by his underlying desire to "*want to believe*?" Or is he simply enamored with the complete impossibility of such knowledge, being captured by such an impossible pursuit?

Those are serious questions. Why indeed would an atheist commit to a purely *physical existence*, then insist on further inquiry about *spiritual things*? (Perhaps if you know such a person, it would be good to ask him why he is interested in asking you about your faith.)

Therefore, atheist demands for proof are unreasonable. A human's physical form precludes his full knowledge of things beyond his physical plane of existence. Thus, no human could fully know all the answers which might be demanded by an atheist. Moreover, even if a person had complete knowledge of tesseract planes of existence, it is most likely he would not possess the language to adequately describe those things. And, even if he tried to explain those things to a skeptic, would the skeptic accept his words?

Faith is Based on One's *Desire to Believe*—Nothing Further

When declaring we believe simply because *we want to believe*, it allows us to bypass all debates.

And, more importantly, such faith is completely sincere, honest and heartfelt. Thus, *childlike faith* is the purest form of faith to which we should aspire.

In Claims #17-21 below, I present childlike faith as the persevering form of Biblical belief. When a person believes *like a child*, his faith is unshakable!

Enjoy! . . .

Claim #17
The <u>undefeatable</u> position: "Faith is believing because *I want to believe.*"

Discussion

If you want to end all debates with atheism, hold fast to this intellectually honest position: *"Faith is believing because I desire to believe."*

Another way of putting this would be to say: *"I believe because I want to believe"* or *"I believe this because it makes me feel good."*

These are all *subjective* statements which have no need to be defended to another person.

And these statements are true—helping you to stay connected to your own heart. After all, it is okay for you to believe something because it makes you feel good!

Who is anyone to tell you what you can and cannot think within your own mind?

Once a person understands this, all debates about religion are gone. *Poof!*

A person is free to hold a belief in his heart: No justification/proof/rationale required.
It doesn't matter what another person thinks about his beliefs. He simply believes because *he wants to believe*.

And, remarkably, this perspective returns religious belief back to its roots...

Remember what we discussed on page 29. Faith does not require proof. So, simply *choosing to believe* is the foundational form of faith. Truly, this is how our ancestors believed.
And, this type of simple faith is the exact pattern taught by the Lord Jesus (Matt. 18:1-5).

Claim #18
Childlike faith gives intellectual freedom to hear others and simply share your faith.

Discussion
This is an important point, and when you understand it, it provides *intellectual freedom*.

Think about it. . . .

I believe something because I desire to believe it.

When this is true, it means I no longer need to "believe" something just because it "makes sense." In this way, faith transcends debate—because, even if I concede a point, my "desire" exists independently.

I can believe *what I want* within my heart, and even if someone makes a good counter point, it doesn't affect my heart. After all, my beliefs are not based on popular opinion or convincing arguments. Rather, my heartfelt beliefs are based on my love for God. And, no one can take that away from me. In this way, heartfelt, childlike faith is *completely immune to anything the world throws at it!*

For example, let's say I am listening to an atheist present biological details—which he says demonstrate evolutionary links between various animals.

When I understand my personal faith is based on *my own desire*, I am free to enjoy listening to the atheist's discussion on biology—simply acknowledging that is how he *chooses* to see the world for himself. But my faith is maintained separate from my physical brain—which "concedes" points and assents to counter-views.

In other words, I can listen to an atheist, and perhaps maybe even agree to "some" of his points—yet I would not yield my faith on the basis of that assent.

I choose to believe in something *because I desire to do so*. I do not believe in something as a result of "proofs." Therefore, no "proofs" can un-do my heartfelt faith.

Faith: No Proof Required

Get it?

So, what makes me different?

Whereas a Christian apologist would be inclined to resist *all points* offered by an atheist in order to maintain the "proofs" for his belief; I am free to concede points with it having <u>*zero effect*</u> on my *heartfelt* beliefs. Moreover, my philosophy of faith—as based on personal desire—remains unassailable by any amount of proofs, no matter how logical or whatever.

Therefore, my position allows me complete intellectual honesty. I can fully maintain my heart faith while assenting to "some" counter-points which make sense.

Guided by this perspective on faith, I often enjoy listening to counter-viewpoints because *I am free to see things from other people's perspectives*. Childlike faith grants me freedom to listen.

But any Christian whose spiritual worldview *relies on proofs* must keep himself under constant pressure to hold those proofs together. Therefore, the Christian with *adult-like* faith may tend to avoid counter-views which might challenge his system of "proofs." And, if a Christian's beliefs are based on "proof," he will be inclined to reject any *atheist counter-proof*—because it endangers the proof-based foundation of his adult-like faith.

The person with *adult-like faith* must maintain his "proofs" like a fragile *house of cards*. He must defend the delicate structure of his house of cards—because removing a single card threatens the entire structure.

But a person with *childlike faith* has no such stress to maintain a *house of cards*. The person with childlike faith simply chooses to believe—and that belief is stored deep within his "heart" . . . immune to any threat. Whereas adult-like faith can be threatened; childlike faith is beyond the reach of all physical things.

So, simply *do* what Jesus *told us to do* . . .

Believe with childlike faith.

Simply declare you *believe the Bible because you want to believe the Bible*. Then you will be free to hear the perspectives of others—recognizing their "arguments" are not capable of changing your heartfelt faith.

When speaking with an atheist you won't need to feel like you have to power him into accepting your "proofs" while he does the same to you.

Rather, if you have childlike faith, you could simply discuss your heartfelt faith, just like this . . .

"I believe in Jesus because it is encouraging to think about God loving me so much He died for me."

You see?

No one could *debate* that because you are free to say what "encourages" you!

A skeptic might say, "I don't believe there was *a Jesus*."
And, your answer would be, "*I do believe!*"

It is that simple.

Your faith in this regard would not rely on "proof" for the *historic* Jesus but on the *encouragement* the story provides to you.
Sure, you might find arguments for the historicity of Jesus interesting, but your faith does not depend on any of those ideas. Instead, your faith depends only on your *desire to believe*—as you feel God's Spirit interacting with your heart.

No "proof" is required.

Do you see the power in this?

Can you imagine what it would be like to live like this—immune to anything which could be said by another? You could focus on sharing your *heart* with people, rather than feeling compelled to list historical "facts."

One could say, quite truthfully, this is the pathway to *incredible faith*—which enables us to persevere all things.

The problem is Christians have been told so often their faith depends on "proof," when it does not. Your faith depends on your *desire to believe*—your choice to follow God's leading. And no amount of arguments or counter-proofs can take away such powerfully *simple* faith.

Therefore, choose to have faith like a child—because you *want to believe*.

Don't have *stuffy ol' grandpa 1,001 reasons* faith. The pathway to freedom is <u>*simple, childlike faith*</u>. The pathway to being a stuffy ol' curmudgeon is to develop a "bazillion" different proofs to pummel opponents.

Just be a *heartfelt* believer who maintains *heartfelt* beliefs—untouchable by the nonsense of the world. And, simply <u>*share your heart*</u> with others.

Claim #19
The persevering position: Faith is "believing because *I want to believe*."

Discussion
Since a foundational characteristic of Christians is that they persevere all things in faith, this means their faith rests solely upon their *desire* to have faith.

Another way of putting this . . .

Imagine a person showed you stacks of books which claim to "disprove" everything about the Bible. Would you get rid of your faith because of what some books say?

Of course you wouldn't—if you are a Christian like the Bible describes. Since the faith of a true Christian is defined by the Bible as a faith that endures to the end, for you to be a proper Christian would require you to side with your faith regardless of any "proof."

For this reason, your faith does not depend on "proof"—*in any way*. Now you may think it does, but it really doesn't. Even if "proofs" were "disproven," you would choose to persevere in your faith because you "desire to do so."

Get it?

Therefore, it is most honest for you to say:

"I believe in Christ because I want to believe in Christ."

And there is nothing wrong with this statement!

You are free, my friend, to believe in your heart what you desire to believe. No one has the right to tell you what you must believe or must not.

So, rather than saying you believe for a certain *reason*, start telling people you believe because you *"want to believe."*

Claim #20
The <u>unassailable</u> position: Faith is "believing because *I want to believe*."

Discussion

In these claims, I present faith as unashamedly subjective and personal—existing independent of any external "proofs."

And, this type of faith is sufficient to guide me in all my life. I simply uphold the story of Jesus in my heart. No additional "proof" is required for this simple, Bible-based belief.

This type of faith is unassailable. When Christians begin articulating their faith in this way, atheists no longer have the ability to debate those *personal* beliefs.

In other words, when a Christian says he believes then shares a heartfelt, personal story, there is nothing for a skeptic to assault. Then the atheist views the faith of the Christian as a unique *personal perspective*—rather than something to argue.

After all, isn't this the whole point of faith?

Shouldn't faith be rooted deep within the *heart* of a person?

Thus, we see faith should be childlike, heartfelt and persevering—based solely upon how the believer has been *personally touched by God*.

Therefore, when asked by an atheist to explain our faith, we should be more mindful to hold fast to this simplicity, stating clearly:

"I love Jesus because He loves me!"

Now, that love of Christ does not need to be *proven*. Rather it is something experienced *within the heart* of the believer.

So, the next time you are asked to *explain your faith*, be ready to give a heartfelt testimony rather than a list of cold "facts." Remove the intellectualism and allow yourself to feel your heart beating. By doing so, you will communicate "faith" which transcends all debates and arguments.

Childlike faith is absolutely transcendent.

Claim #21
Childlike faith is the model of Biblical faith (Matt. 18:2-4)

Discussion
Note the simplicity in all my claims—where I unashamedly present my "desire to believe." This is childlike faith—which requires no "proof" beyond itself.

Now, here's the question . . .

Do you have *childlike faith*, or do you have *adult-like faith*?

When the Bible tells you to simply *believe*, are you inclined to try to make faith into this high-minded, intellectual enterprise?

I'm not telling you what to believe, but if you are in the process of doing a spiritual inventory, please allow me to coach you through this process . . .

For example, you are much better off if you simply say, "*I believe in the Flood because I want to*," rather than saying, "*I believe in the Flood because of (x)(y)(z).*"

Keep it simple.

Be honest with yourself.

If you never intend to abandon your belief in the Flood, then don't mislead yourself into thinking you believe it because of "proofs"—which could one day be *disproven*. Then, if ever (x)(y)(z) are disproven, and you maintain your belief in the Flood, you will find you have been dishonest to yourself—having claimed those were the "reasons" why you held that belief in the Flood.

Make sense?

Therefore, take the childlike faith approach . . .

Simply say you believe in the Flood *because you want to believe* in it. That way, no amount of proofs could ever dissuade you from your belief (because your belief is based on your heart, not proofs).

Easy peasy.

So, do you have *adult-like* faith? Or do you have *childlike* faith? Is your faith stored within your *brain* or in your *heart*?

Cast off earthly expectations for proof and embrace Jesus in your heart—with childlike faith.

Genesis Pilgrim

How to Share Your Faith

So, what advice could be offered to a person venturing to share his faith with others?

Keep it simple and heartfelt.

When sharing your faith, you do not need to offer lists of "proofs" and "facts." Instead, simply explain what is *in your heart*.

To do this, ask yourself what "inspires" you. Then share those heartfelt inspirations with other people. By doing this you will simply communicate your heart with others.

So, *how* could you do this?

To help you understand *how to share your faith*, I will present a series of "examples" below (Examples #1-8). For each "example" picture yourself simply saying *something like this* to another person.

Of course, there are countless things one could say to another person when sharing his faith. But these *examples* should get you on the right path—helping you to consider the simplicity involved in sharing heartfelt, childlike faith.

Enjoy! . . .

How to Share Your Faith
Example #1
Say this: *"I believe in the Bible because I enjoy reading it."*

Discussion

There are many things I could say about the Bible—detailing how it has enhanced my life. Being a meticulous person, I appreciate the Bible for its depth and many different perspectives. I have enjoyed reading it for so many years. And I can always search for something which previously escaped my notice.

Therefore, within my heart, my *belief in the Bible* rests solely on *how I relate to it*. No one can take that from me. Nor do I need to "prove" how I feel to another person.

Note to "*support my belief in the Bible,*" I did not cite manuscript numbers, historic details or anything like that.

Of course, I could. But that is not where my faith rests—with external details. Instead, my faith rests *on the Bible itself.* Sure, the external details can be interesting, but my belief in the Bible does not depend on anything beyond the Bible itself. Therefore, I say unashamedly:

"I believe in the Bible *because I enjoy reading it.*

If a skeptic were to challenge my statement, I guess he could say, "*Well, you enjoy reading other things, don't you? So why not base your beliefs on other books?*"

And, if pressed by such questions, I could subjectively respond: Saying I *choose* to hold the Bible as superior to all other books *because I want to*.

No further explanation is required.

Therefore, heartfelt belief in the Bible requires "no proof." If one desires to uphold the Bible in his heart, he is free to do so.

No "proof" required.

Rather than bantering with a skeptic about the historicity of the Bible, or ancient manuscript numbers, I can simply share the Bible stories which have inspired me.

For example, I could discuss a story from the Gospel of John—explaining how it has given me courage to face challenges in my life. To do so I do not need to *historically prove* the Gospel of John or the Bible because my faith does not rely on "proving" it historically.

Rather, my belief in the Bible is based on *my heartfelt connection to what it says*. And this is something which cannot be taken away from me.

Get it?

How to Share Your Faith Example #2
Say this: "*I believe in the Creation story because I like it.*"

Discussion

Note in the above statement I did not declare "proofs" for creation. Nor do I need to state proofs. I simply stated, "*I believe in the Creation story because I like it.*"

I find the Genesis story interesting and I am encouraged by the thought of God carefully creating all things in order.

In order to maintain this personal belief, I do not need to list off biological facts, facts about the "planets," geography facts or anything at all. My faith does not depend on any of those things.

Instead, my faith rests solely on *the Genesis story itself*: I heard the story; I like the story. Therefore, I uphold the story as precious in my heart.

This is an unassailable position.

Moreover, my position most closely mirrors the position of Bible faith—because it is heartfelt, sincere and simple.

I'll put it this way . . .

Do you think Moses needed to examine *rock stratification* to "prove" his belief in creation?

Or do you think Moses needed to read a textbook on sedimentation to convince himself of the flood?

Think about it.

Of course, such ideas are ridiculous.

Instead, Moses—and all the ancient people in the Bible—simply *chose to believe*. No additional "proof" was required beyond *their own desire to believe*.

Now, imagine I were to say to a skeptic: "*I believe in the creation story because I like it.*"

By doing so, I completely bypass any requirement to cite "proofs" for the Bible.

After all, no matter what "proofs" against creation I am presented, *I will always maintain my belief in creation*. So, to be true to myself, I simply state, "*I believe in creation because I like it.*"

I believe in creation because *I want to* believe in creation.

Get it?

How to Share Your Faith Example #3

Say this: *"I believe in the Flood because I want to believe in the Flood."*

Discussion

This position, however rudimentary, is <u>superior</u> to other positions which require "proof." In fact, this is an example of heartfelt, childlike faith—the kind which the Lord Jesus upheld as ideal (Matt. 18:1-5).

And, therefore, this simple claim is better than all claims which are based on "proof."

Consider the following . . .

Imagine a person said, "I believe in the Flood because of geographical evidence."

This would be an intellectually dishonest position—because *I guarantee his faith itself does not depend on geographical information.* In other words, even if one's "geographical evidence" were disproven, he would still maintain his belief.

Furthermore, should we be so unwise to allow our hearts to be governed by geographical textbooks?

Thus, a believer's faith depends *on his own desire to believe something*—not "facts" or "proof."

Therefore, unashamedly say what you mean: "*I believe in the Flood because I want to.*"

Beliefs should always bring us back to our hearts. Your faith is based on your "belief"—and nothing further. This is a good thing!
After all, doesn't the Bible call us to simply believe—with the faith of a child?

How many children do you know who believe in the Flood because of *geographical proofs*? Don't children believe simply because they *desire to believe*?

Likewise, you should simply believe what you *desire to believe*—no strings attached. You should simply believe because *you want to believe.*

How to Share Your Faith Example #4

Say this: *"I believe in angels because it helps me when I am scared."*

Discussion

This is another subjective claim which is incredibly powerful—and intellectually honest. I simply state: *"I enjoy thinking about the protection angels provide me when I am scared."*

No "proof" is required to support this statement because it is completely personal. It is heartfelt, sincere and simple.

Furthermore, this perspective most closely aligns to the teachings of the Bible—where people *assumed the existence of angels* (as in the book of Hebrews).

Now, you will not find in the Bible a list of "proofs" to demonstrate the existence of angels. Rather, the writers of the Bible *just believe in the existence of angels* and speak to their readers as if they all likewise *believe in angels*.

Throughout *all* human history, our ancestors didn't require "proof" for such things—they *simply chose to believe*.

So, are you seeing how ridiculous it is to demand "proof" from the Bible—when not even the writers of the Bible held themselves to that standard?

Could you imagine a skeptic saying to the writer of Hebrews: "*I need you to show me physical proof for the existence of angels?*"

It was accepted throughout human history that humans are free to believe within their hearts. It would make no sense for a skeptic to require physical "proof" for spiritual things.

After all, the whole point of the Bible is centered upon *faith*. We are called to walk by faith, not by sight (2 Cor. 5:7).

So, would the God of the Bible be pleased by a person who believes only because of what is physically shown to him?

Indeed, God would recoil from such a person—whose heart is obstinate and whose faith is only based on *physical* acquiescence to *physical* "proofs," being governed by his adult-like brain rather than childlike humility.

So, what would be the point of offering "physical proof" to a skeptic, even if you had "physical proof?"

Would such "physical proof" result in the birthing of sincere, childlike faith in the heart of the skeptic?

At most, it would produce only a lukewarm "believer" who is anchored to the *physical* world—citing *physical* objects as the source of his new beliefs. And, since his faith is grounded in only "physical proofs," he could be tossed aside readily by any argument which sufficiently set aside that "proof."

Decide for yourself . . .

Would God be pleased with such worldly faith?

Therefore, childlike faith aligns more closely with faith declared in the Bible.
The Bible is not concerned with forcing skeptical people to concede to "facts." Instead, the Bible encourages people to believe with childlike faith (Matt. 18:1-5).

How to Share Your Faith Example #5
Say this: *"I believe in the spiritual world because it is interesting and helpful."*

Discussion

In my book, <u>Survival of the Superstitious: How Religion Helped Ancient Humans Survive</u>, I explain how *all* ancient human societies were religious. I put forth the idea that religion (in general) was the premiere means through which ancient people found joy in their otherwise dull lives—spurring them to creativity and abstract thinking necessary to the development of nearly every aspect of society.

I note how ancient humans would gather to tell stories. And, in these gatherings, people united with one another in shared values as they established standards for their clans through stories.

Likewise, I find today that dwelling on thoughts of the spiritual world is *still helpful*. When trapped in mundane situations, I find it invigorating to use my mind to picture spiritual things.

Can I be faulted for this when ancient humans—during time immemorial—have *all* done the same things, using their minds to picture spiritual things?

In the midst of a 21st Century world, where skeptics deride those with spiritual beliefs, it is important to be mindful of humanity's past.
Humans *enjoy* believing in spiritual things! We always have. Likewise, in the present time we are free to fix our hearts on spiritual things.

In this way, my spiritual beliefs are immune to requirements for "proof." I am free to believe in spiritual things because *I find them interesting and helpful*. I don't need to justify my beliefs to another person.

Faith = No "proof" required.

How to Share Your Faith Example #6

Say this: *"I believe in the story of Jesus because it is my favorite story."*

Discussion

Note in the above claim I *simply* state my personal preference—saying the story of Jesus it is my "favorite" story. In other words, for me, the story of Jesus is the Greatest Story Ever Told.

The story of Jesus leads me to simply reflect on God's love for me. Christ loves me so much He chose to offer His life in exchange for me (John 3:16).

Therefore, I can say, "*I believe in the gospel of Jesus because it is my favorite story.*"

And, interestingly, this "claim" is unassailable because it is based on nothing beyond *my own desire*. It neither needs to be defended, nor can it be defended.

That *belief* is simply that . . . a *belief*. It is purely subjective and personal—and wonderfully so.

No one could take this away from me. Nor could another "prove" I am "wrong" for upholding this story.

<u>*I am free to believe!*</u>

In the justification of your own faith, I encourage you to take a similar approach. Simply state why you hold a belief precious in your heart and no one can take it away from you.

There is no need for you to cite "proof" for your beliefs.

Your heart is free.

Faith = No proof required.

How to Share Your Faith Example #7
Say this: *"I believe in the resurrection of Jesus because it is inspiring."*

Discussion

The idea of Christ offering Himself to save me is humbling. And, the idea of Jesus holding power over death is invigorating. It gives me courage to face whatever stands before me—confident Jesus will guard me in every hardship.

Moreover, like all my subjective statements, this statement is unassailable. It neither needs to be defended, nor can it really be defended—because it is rooted in my own subjective heart.

To the person who holds such a position, it doesn't matter whether I can find the *exact* stone which was rolled over the Lord's grave, or the nails from His cross.

Like my countless ancient ancestors, I am free to believe *what I desire*. I don't need to go to the original locations or examine copies of the documents which attest to such things.

None of those things matter—because regardless of anything physical—I choose to hold "belief" in my heart. So, any "proof" in favor or against the resurrection is completely irrelevant to such faith.

It just doesn't matter.

I am free to believe in the resurrection because *I want to* believe in the resurrection.

I do not need to "prove" the resurrection. I simply hear and believe—with childlike faith.

No proof required.

How to Share Your Faith Example #8
Say this: *"I believe in the afterlife because I am encouraged by its provision of justice."*

Discussion
It is apparent many people escape justice in this world—whether for good or evil. I find my belief in the afterlife encouraging because God will mete out everything in *total justice*.

The thought of the perfect God overseeing justice is helpful—making sense of pain and suffering in this world.

A person could ask me to "prove" my belief in the afterlife, but there is nothing to "prove." I only state my *encouragement* in the concept of afterlife. I don't need to *prove* the afterlife itself. So, by making a subjective statement—where I focus on my own "encouragement"—I remove myself from any reasonable requirement to provide "proof."

I am free to believe in the afterlife because *I want to* believe in the afterlife.

I don't need to cite examples of "near-death" experiences or anything like that.

I simply believe in Heaven with childlike faith.

No proof required.

My heart requires no stamp of validation from skeptics, nor society.

<u>I am free to believe</u>.

Faith: No Proof Required

Conclusions

In this book, my main point is that people are *free to believe*. Their hearts are not governed by others. A person can believe as *he desires to believe*.

However, when realizing this, it leads us into a problem. . . .

Since people are "free to believe," <u>what</u> should they believe? Should a person believe in anything?

I think not.

Although people are free to make their own decisions, I think it wise to provide some basic guidelines. So, please consider my final "claim" . . .

Claim #22
The best beliefs are *time-tested* and *trustworthy*.

Discussion
Of course, people are free to believe whatever they desire. They are the kings of their own hearts. So, a person can uphold *whatever they want* within themselves. We know this is true—because people believe all types of things.

But if you are a person on a quest to define *your beliefs*, let me encourage you to consider believing something "trustworthy."

What do I mean?

Well, in the 21st Century, I am sure we can find people who believe in *anything*. So, when you choose your own belief system, maybe you could start—like me—by considering others who hold such beliefs.

For me personally, I give higher credibility to belief systems which are **time-tested**. In other words, if a certain belief system was held by your ancestors, and helped them to survive, then perhaps it would be best for you to begin by considering that belief system.

This is a reason why I uphold the Bible. I enjoy reading about the many people in the Bible who endured hardship through faith (Heb. 11). Therefore, since the faith of the Bible was capable of sustaining the people in the Bible, I know this faith is capable of sustaining me.

Could such faith likewise benefit you? Decide for yourself.

Determine if a system of belief has been **successful at creating and maintaining human societies**.

In my studies, what I find most remarkable is the fact that all ancient human societies were religious; whereas atheism has *never* produced an enduring society. In other words, human history teaches atheism is a dead end; whereas belief in religion at least gives societies a *chance* for survival.

Likewise, in your quest to determine *what to believe*, perhaps you would be wise to consider granting priority to belief systems which have proven *most effective* at producing and maintaining societies.

So, in your personal quest, consider belief systems which are **time-tested** and **trustworthy**. Don't be deceived into believing things which are proven "dead ends."

Thus, if you follow these guidelines, I am convinced you will be led—like me—to carefully consider the Bible. And, if you put your faith in the Bible's teachings, you will join with a successful group of believers spanning millennia (Heb. 11). Therefore, the past success record of the Bible establishes it as time-tested and trustworthy.

"I believe in the Bible because I think it is time-tested and trustworthy. So, I trust the Bible with my heart."

Faith = No Proof Required

Heartfelt, childlike faith does not place its hope in physical things. In fact, faith does not rely on *anything* physical—except maybe the pinging of my brain cells as I think about my faith! Beyond that *nothing physical* is required.

A believer does not need a list of physical facts to support his heart. Rather, he <u>*chooses to believe*</u>—and that heartfelt belief is based purely on his personal connection to God. Nothing physical is required.

Whereas others would be inclined to offer physical "proof" for their faith; childlike faith invites us to boldly declare: "*I believe in the story of Jesus because it inspires me.*"

There are many ways I could re-phrase this, but ultimately childlike faith is grounded *only* in the subjective desire of one's heart.

One of the greatest strengths of childlike faith is its honesty. A man with childlike, heartfelt faith has no requirement to review archaeological facts to uphold his beliefs. He bears no requirement to review historical records buried in the Vatican. Nor does his faith require him to travel to Israel to do archaeological excavations. Heartfelt faith relies on none of those things.

And, in fact, heartfelt faith relies on nothing in our physical plane of existence whatsoever. Childlike, heartfelt faith is based only on one's subjective mind and personal choice—as the heart of the believer is touched by God.

Jesus told His followers they should have childlike faith—where they simply *choose* to believe. And when reading the Bible, we see it invites people to simply *choose* to "believe" (John 20:31).

Bible faith involves a simple childlike choice to believe. In the Bible we will not find complicated requirements for Christians to use "science" or lists of facts to "prove" their beliefs. In the Bible we are never told we must dig up rocks, raid tombs or date dusty manuscripts. A person simply *chooses to believe*—and that process is independent of physical proof.

Nor does childlike faith require approval from others. In our Western societies we are conditioned to think everything can be "voted" upon and that popular "vote" determines truth. But this does not apply to the hearts of people—who freely choose for themselves what they desire to hold precious.

And, most remarkably, when one understands his faith does not rely on physical things, then nothing in the physical world can remove that faith. My heart can always uphold its own belief. Therefore, there is nothing in the physical plane of existence which could remove my faith.

In this way, childlike faith has the ability to "persevere" all things; whereas adult-like faith is tossed about whenever it is brought to consider "new facts" or "proofs."

So, if you want faith which perseveres all things, your best hope is *childlike, heartfelt faith*.

Faith which is beyond everything physical cannot be shaken by anything physical.

I don't need the "world" to tell me if my beliefs are "true" or not. It doesn't matter if the world validates my beliefs.

In fact, Christ told us that our beliefs would run contrary to the fallen world—so indeed we should expect that the world will ever stand against the hearts of the faithful.

Therefore, the whole point of heartfelt religion is *subjectivity*. To hold a belief does not require public assent. The person simply *chooses to believe*!

Belief occurs as the heart of the man is touched by God. So, only those two parties are necessary: *God and the believer*. The opinions, thoughts, questions and objections of the *peanut gallery* are moot.

When God is invited within a person's heart, it doesn't matter what the world thinks about it!

My beliefs are within my heart. And that is all I need. That is the whole point of childlike faith.

So, I can say to you, "*I believe in Jesus because I want to believe in Jesus!*"

No extra "proof" is required.

Faith = No Proof Required (2 Cor. 5:7).

Faith: No Proof Required

For more titles, check out www.GenesisPilgrim.com

www.ingramcontent.com/pod-product-compliance
Lightning Source LLC
Chambersburg PA
CBHW071504040426
42444CB00008B/1480